SATURDAY SWEATERS

Saturday
Sweaters

Easy to Knit, Easy to Wear

Doreen L. Marquart

Saturday Sweaters: Easy to Knit, Easy to Wear
© 2005 by Doreen L. Marquart

Martingale® & COMPANY

Martingale & Company
20205 144th Avenue NE
Woodinville, WA 98072-8478 USA
www.martingale-pub.com

Credits

President .... Nancy J. Martin
CEO .... Daniel J. Martin
VP and General Manager .... Tom Wierzbicki
Publisher .... Jane Hamada
Editorial Director .... Mary V. Green
Managing Editor .... Tina Cook
Technical Editor .... Darilyn Page
Copy Editor .... Ellen Balstad
Design Director .... Stan Green
Illustrator .... Robin Strobel
Cover and Text Designer .... Stan Green
Studio Photographer .... Brent Kane
Fashion Photographer .... John P. Hamel
Fashion Stylist .... Pamela Simpson
Hairstylist and Makeup Artist ...... Lori Smith

Printed in China
10 09 08 07 06 05   8 7 6 5 4 3 2 1

Mission Statement

Dedicated to providing quality products and service to inspire creativity.

Library of Congress Cataloging-in-Publication Data

Marquart, Doreen L.
    Saturday sweaters : easy to knit, easy to wear / Doreen L. Marquart.
        p. cm.
    ISBN 1-56477-605-0
    1. Knitting—Patterns. 2. Sweaters. I. Title.
    TT825.M2758 2005
    746.43'20432—dc22
                                            2005008703

Dedication

To my husband, Gordon, for your continuous support, encouragement, and faith in me and my abilities. And to my three sons, Michael, Phillip, and Cody. Through watching you grow and fulfill your dreams, I learned what my own dreams were and that it is never too late to follow them. Without the four of you, this book would never have become a reality. I love you all.

Acknowledgments

I'd like to thank the following:

My faithful customers, who are first and foremost my friends. I'm just happy to be the one who supplies you with the necessities for your addiction! Without your willingness and eagerness to share ideas for the type of sweaters you were looking for, this project would never have become a reality.

All the yarn companies who furnished materials for the sweaters in this book. Thank you for providing me with such luscious yarns. You are all great to work with.

Martingale & Company—thank you for taking a chance with me and guiding me through the process of making my first book.

ENTS

Introduction

I have always found comfort in my knitting—it helps me relax, relieves the pressures of the day, takes my mind away from what is going on in my nonknitting life, and just plain makes me feel good.

This became of the utmost importance when my husband spent 30 days in the hospital during the fall of 2003. I found I needed something to knit while I was visiting him, waiting for tests to be done and surgeries to be performed. Since I was not exactly in the state of mind to handle anything too complex, my project had to be rather mindless. It had to be something I could knit while visiting with him that would help me relax, yet not put me to sleep if I worked on it during some of those long, quiet evenings I had by myself at home. It had to comfort me.

I had those same goals in mind when I began to design sweaters for this book. I also decided that I wanted the sweaters to be the type that you would grab first when you went to your closet. I wanted them to be the sweaters that you would live in, the ones that would make the day better just because you had them on, and become your *comfort* sweaters. I wanted them to be not only a comfort to make but a comfort to wear.

As I continued in the design process, I discovered that my sweaters also served another purpose. As a shop owner I often get beginner knitters who are looking for sweater patterns they can make when they are ready to move beyond scarves. The designs in this book lend themselves perfectly for first sweater projects. There are new techniques to learn, but the designs are not so overwhelming as to scare off the novice.

Thus, I designed this book with two types of knitters in mind. These are sweaters for beginners to use as their first step out of the scarf-only world, and for more advanced knitters to use to give their brain a break.

The designs in this book are meant to be fun and easy to knit while also being sweaters that you'll absolutely love to wear.

Abbreviations

approx	approximately	P	purl
beg	beginning	patt	pattern
BO	bind off	P2tog	purl 2 stitches together
A	color A	PM	place marker
B	color B	psso	pass slipped stitch(es) over
C	color C	PU	pick up and knit
ch	chain	pw	purlwise
CO	cast on	rem	remaining
cont	continue	rep	repeat
dec	decrease	RH	right hand
dpn(s)	double-pointed needle(s)	rnd(s)	round(s)
EOR	every other row	RS	right side(s)
est	established	sc	single crochet
foll	follow(ing)	sl	slip
g	gram(s)	SSK	slip 1, slip 1, knit these 2
garter st	garter stitch		stitches together
inc	increase(ing)	st(s)	stitch(es)
K	knit	St st	stockinette stitch
K2tog	knit 2 stitches together	tbl	through the back loop
kw	knitwise	tog	together
LH	left hand	WS	wrong side(s)
M1	make 1 stitch	wyif	with yarn in front
MC	main color	yds	yards
oz	ounces	YO	yarn over

Standard Yarn-Weight System

In this book, project yarns are labeled with yarn-weight categories compiled by the Craft Yarn Council of America. Refer to the chart below for descriptions of the various categories.

Yarn-Weight Symbol and Category Names	1 SUPER FINE	2 FINE	3 LIGHT	4 MEDIUM	5 BULKY	6 SUPER BULKY
Types of Yarns in Category	Sock, Fingering, Baby	Sport, Baby	DK, Light Worsted	Worsted, Afghan, Aran	Chunky, Craft, Rug	Bulky, Roving
Knit Gauge Range in Stockinette Stitch to 4"	27 to 32 sts	23 to 26 sts	21 to 24 sts	16 to 20 sts	12 to 15 sts	6 to 11 sts
Recommended Needle in Metric Size Range	2.25 to 3.25 mm	3.25 to 3.75 mm	3.75 to 4.5 mm	4.5 to 5.5 mm	5.5 to 8 mm	8 mm and larger
Recommended Needle in U.S. Size Range	1 to 3	3 to 5	5 to 7	7 to 9	9 to 11	11 and larger

Insert a third needle, the same size or one size larger than the project needle, into the first stitch on each of the left-hand needles. Knit the stitches together creating 1 stitch. Knit the next 2 stitches together in the same manner. Bind off 1 stitch from the right-hand needle.

Continue working across the row, knitting 1 stitch from the front together with 1 stitch from the back. Each time you have 2 stitches on the right-hand needle, bind 1 off. When you get down to 1 stitch, cut the yarn and pull it through and secure the tail of the yarn.

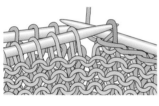

Knit together one stitch from front needle and one stitch from back needle.

Bind off.

Picking Up Stitches

To pick up stitches for the neckband, divide the neck opening into 4 sections. Divide the number of stitches you have to pick up by 4 and pick up that number of stitches in each section. This method assures that the stitches are evenly spaced.

To pick up the stitches, go under both strands of the edge stitch. If you go through only the very outside loop, the neckband will be uneven and there will be holes around the neck of your sweater. Stitches need to be evenly spaced. Since the number of stitches

per row is not the same as stitches per inch, you may have to make some adjustments when picking up stitches. You do not need to pick up a stitch in every space across. Pick the stitches up evenly around the neckline of the sweater.

Should a particular stitch appear loose or leave a hole, you can knit this stitch through the back loop to tighten up the stitch and prevent a hole.

Single Crochet Edging

Make a slip knot and place it on your hook. Insert your hook into the first stitch, going under two strands to prevent any holes. Wrap the yarn over the crochet hook and pull through. You now should have 2 loops on the hook. Wrap the yarn over the hook again and pull through both stitches on the hook, leaving 1 stitch on the hook.

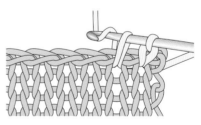

Insert hook into stitch, yarn over hook, pull loop through to front, yarn over hook.

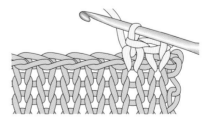

Pull loop through both loops on hook.

Backward Crochet Edging (Reverse Crochet, Crab Stitch, Knurl Stitch)

This is a particularly nice way to edge knitting. It gives a finished look without adding too much length to the garment. Please note that the backward crochet edging will need to be removed should you later decide to add a different edge to your sweater, since this stitch creates a finished border.

Select a hook size that is appropriate for the yarn you are using. With the right side facing you, work a row of single crochet evenly across the area you'll be applying the border to. You may have to skip a stitch here and there to make sure that the work lies flat. If you need to go around a corner, put 2 or 3 single crochet stitches in the very corner stitch. When you have a row of single crochet around the edge, make 1 single crochet but *do not turn* your work. If you are working in the round, join with a slip stitch to the first single crochet. *Remember not to turn your work.*

Working in the direction opposite from what you normally do, work a second row of single crochet over the foundation row you just made. Notice that you have a lovely row of loops that are going tightly over the top of the crocheting. If your loops are uneven, try again. This technique takes a little practice but is well worth the effort.

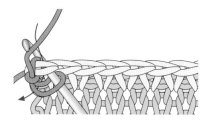

Join yarn with slip stitch. Insert hook into first stitch to the right.

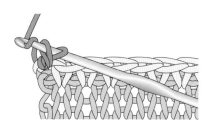

Yarn over hook, pull through both loops on hook, keeping hook parallel to work.

Assembly

While there are many different methods for sewing seams, this method adds virtually no bulk. If the seam you are sewing together is a side edge, go through the very outside strand of yarn. If it is a bound-off edge, go through both strands of that stitch. *Weave back and forth.* (The side the needle comes out from is the side you go into for the next stitch.) This makes a nice, flat seam. Note that sometimes on one side you'll be working with bound-off stitches while on the other side of the seam you may have side stitches. You'll be going under the very outside strand on one side but under both strands of the bound-off stitch on the other.

Flat Sleeve Assembly

This technique works great for sewing sleeves that were knit flat onto the body section that was also knit flat. Measure and place a marker on both the front and back sections at the depth of the sleeve as given in the beginning of the pattern directions. Find the center point of the sleeve and place another marker.

Place the right side of the sleeve together with the right side of the body, matching up the shoulder seam with the center sleeve marker, and the sleeve edges with the markers you placed for sleeve depth. Pin the sleeve into place.

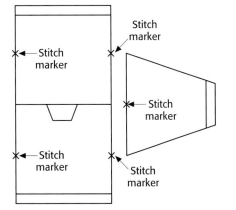

Thread a piece of yarn, or the tail left from the bind off of the sleeve, onto a tapestry needle. Attach the sleeve to the body by weaving the yarn back and forth. It works best to go through both sides of the bind-off stitch on the sleeve and the outside loop of the stitch on the body. It is essential to maintain an even tension so that your seam doesn't pucker or have holes. You'll find that you need to go through each bind-off stitch of the sleeve but you do not have to go through every stitch on the body section. Line up the sleeve section and go through the stitch on the body that is directly across from it. You'll occasionally skip a stitch on the side section.

Weaving in Ends

Weave in ends for 2" to 3" to make sure that they don't peek back out of your finished sweater. Work down at an angle on the wrong side, going under one strand of each stitch. After about 1½", go up about the same distance in the opposite direction, forming a V. This method holds the ends in place quite nicely as you wear and launder your sweater.

Kitchener Stitch

The kitchener stitch is a type of grafting that is used to join two pieces of knitting together. It is done by creating a row of knitting by hand with a tapestry needle and is completely flat and invisible when complete.

The kitchener stitch was used on this cardigan to make an invisible join where the vertical stripes meet at the shoulder seams.

For the projects in this book, you'll remove the provisional chain and place the *live* stitches onto a knitting needle the same size as your project needles. Each set of stitches from the front and the back go on separate needles.

Hold the needles together in your left hand with the wrong sides of the work together. Thread a piece of yarn on a tapestry needle long enough to work the number of stitches you have on the needles. Make sure you have enough yarn so you don't run out partway through.

First Stitch

Front Needle: Insert the tapestry needle as if to purl that stitch, leave stitch on knitting needle, and pull the yarn through.

Back Needle: Insert the tapestry needle as if to knit that stitch, leave stitch on knitting needle, and pull yarn through.

Remainder of Row until Last Stitch

Front Needle: Insert the tapestry needle as if to knit the first stitch and slip it off onto the tapestry needle. Immediately go through next stitch on the front needle as if to purl, leaving it on knitting needle, and pull the yarn through.

Back Needle: Insert the tapestry needle as if to purl the first stitch and slip it onto the tapestry needle. Immediately go through the next stitch on the back needle as if to knit, leaving it on the knitting needle, and pull the yarn through.

Last Stitch

Front Needle: Insert the tapestry needle as if to knit the stitch and slip it off.

Back Needle: Insert the tapestry needle as if to purl the stitch, slip it off, and pull through.

Weave in the yarn tail on the wrong side.

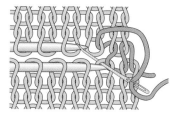

Garter Rib Pullover

This sweater has a lovely bottom band that adds interest without changing the comfortable fit of the sweater.

Finished chest measurement: 38 (40, 43, 45, 47, 49, 51)"

Finished length: 20½ (20½, 20½, 21, 21½, 22½, 23)"

Sleeve drop: 9½ (9½, 9½, 10, 10½, 11, 11)"

Materials

Yarn: 7 (7, 7, 8, 8, 9, 9) skeins of 128 Bulky Tweed from Cascade (3½ oz / 128 yds; 100% wool; color 606), or approx 800 (825, 875, 925, 975, 1025, 1200) yds of bulky-weight yarn ⑤

Needles: 29" circular needle in size 9, or the size required to obtain gauge; 16" circular needle in size 9; dpns in size 9

Notions: St holders, st markers

Gauge

3½ sts and 4½ rows = 1" in St st on size 9 needle

Body

Using the 29" circular needle, CO 132 (140, 148, 156, 164, 172, 180) sts. PM and join. Be careful not to twist the sts.

Bottom Border

Rnds 1, 3, and 5: Knit around.

Rnds 2, 4, and 6: Purl around.

Rnds 7, 9, and 11: Knit around.

Rnds 8, 10, and 12: *K2, P2, rep from * around.

Rnds 13–18: Rep rnds 1–6.

These 18 rows form the bottom edging.

Change to St st (knit every rnd) and cont until piece measures 11 (11, 11, 11, 11, 11½, 12)" or the desired length to armhole.

Back

K66 (70, 74, 78, 82, 86, 90) sts. Place these sts onto holders or a spare needle to use later for the sweater front. Knit across rem 66 (70, 74, 78, 82, 86, 90) sts. Working back and forth, cont in St st (knit on RS, purl on WS) until the back measures 9½ (9½, 9½, 10, 10½, 11, 11)" from the armhole division. Place sts onto 3 holders, divided as follows:

First and third holders: 21 (23, 25, 27, 29, 30, 32) sts each for shoulders

Second holder: 24 (24, 24, 24, 24, 26, 26) sts for back neck

Front

Place the front sts back onto a knitting needle. Attach the yarn and work back and forth in St st until the front measures 3" *shorter* than finished back length, ending with a WS row.

Neck Shaping

K26 (28, 30, 32, 34, 35, 37) sts and place the next 14 (14, 14, 14, 14, 16, 16) sts onto a holder. Attach a 2nd skein of yarn and knit across rem 26 (28, 30, 32, 34, 35, 37) sts. Work 1 row even. Working both sides at the same time, dec 1 st at each neck edge EOR 5 (5, 5, 5, 5, 5, 5) times—21 (23, 25, 27, 29, 30, 32) sts.

■ *To make the neckline lie more smoothly and look more uniform, K2tog for the dec at the left neck edge and SSK for the dec at the right neck edge. Refer to "K2tog" and "SSK" on page 13.*

Work even until the front measures the same as the back. Join the front and the back shoulders using the 3-needle BO. Refer to "Three-Needle Bind Off" on page 13.

Neckband

With RS facing, using the 16" circular needle and starting at the back of the sweater, K24 (24, 24, 24, 24, 26, 26) sts from the holder, PU 15 (15, 15, 15, 15, 15, 15) sts down the left front, K14 (14, 14, 14, 14, 16, 16) sts from the front holder, and PU 15 (15, 15, 15, 15, 15, 15) sts from the right neck front. PM—68 (68, 68, 68, 68, 72, 72) sts.

Rnds 1 and 3: Purl.

Rnd 2: Knit.

Rnd 4: Knit, dec 4 sts evenly around—64 (64, 64, 64, 64, 68, 68) sts.

Rnds 5 and 7: *K2, P2, rep from * around.

Rnd 6: Knit.

Rnd 8: Knit, dec 8 sts evenly—56 (56, 56, 56, 56, 60, 60) sts.

Rnd 9: Purl.

Rnd 10: Knit.

BO loosely pw.

Sleeves

Using dpns, CO 32 (32, 32, 36, 36, 36, 38) sts. PM and join, being careful not to twist the sts. Work 18 rnds in garter st border as for "Body" on page 18. Begin sleeve body as follows, switching to 16" circular needle when you have enough sts to do so.

Knit 1 rnd even. Cont in St st, inc 1 st at each end every 3 rnds 4 (4, 4, 4, 6, 8, 8) times and then every 4 rnds 13 (13, 13, 13, 13, 13, 12) times—66 (66, 66, 70, 74, 78, 78) sts. Work even until piece measures 17 (17½, 17½, 18, 18, 19, 19)" or the desired sleeve length. BO loosely.

■ *Recommended inc: Inc by using the M1 technique **after** the first st of the rnd and another M1 **before** the last st of the rnd. Refer to "Increasing" on page 13.*

Finishing

Sew in the sleeves. Weave in all the loose ends.

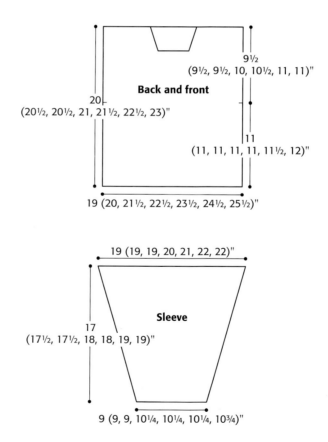

9½
(9½, 9½, 10, 10½, 11, 11)"

Back and front

20
(20½, 20½, 21, 21½, 22½, 23)"

11
(11, 11, 11, 11, 11½, 12)"

19 (20, 21½, 22½, 23½, 24½, 25½)"

19 (19, 19, 20, 21, 22, 22)"

Sleeve

17
(17½, 17½, 18, 18, 19, 19)"

9 (9, 9, 10¼, 10¼, 10¼, 10¾)"

Moss Rib Stitch Pullover

A loose fit along with a sporty-looking stitch makes this pullover a design that you'll love to live in.

Finished chest measurement: 35 (39½, 43, 48, 51)"
Finished length: 22 (22, 23, 23, 24)"
Sleeve drop: 9½ (9½, 10, 10, 11)"

Materials

Yarn: 11 (11, 12, 13, 14) skeins of Silk Garden from Noro (50 g/110 yds; 45% silk/45% kid mohair/10% lamb's wool; color 84) or approx 1110 (1210, 1320, 1430, 1540) yds of worsted-weight yarn ④

Needles: Straight or 24" circular needles in size 7, or the size required to obtain gauge; 16" circular needle in size 7

Notions: St holders, st markers, row markers

Gauge

5 sts and 7 rows = 1" in patt st on size 7 needles

Back

Using the straight or 24" circular needles, CO 87 (99, 107, 119, 127) sts.

Row 1 (RS): K3, *P1, K3, rep from * across row.

Row 2: K1, *P1, K3, rep from * to last 2 sts, P1, K1.

Rep these 2 rows until the back measures 22 (22, 23, 23, 24)" from beg, ending with a WS row. Divide onto 3 st holders as follows:

First and third holders: 29 (35, 39, 42, 46) sts each for shoulders

Second holder: 29 (29, 29, 35, 35) sts for back neck

Front

Work same as the back until the front measures 3" *shorter* than total length of the back, ending with a WS row.

Neck Shaping

Work in patt across 34 (40, 44, 47, 51) sts. Place next 19 (19, 19, 25, 25) sts onto a st holder. Attach a 2nd skein and work in patt across rem 34 (40, 44, 47, 51) sts.

Working both sides at the same time and keeping in patt, dec 1 st on each side of the neck on next RS row and every RS row 5 times—29 (35, 39, 42, 46) sts.

■ *To make the neckline lie more smoothly and look more uniform, K2tog for the dec at the left neck edge and SSK for the dec at the right neck edge. Refer to "K2tog" and "SSK" on page 13.*

Cont even in patt until the front measures the same length as the back from the beg. Join

MOSS RIB STITCH PULLOVER

the front and the back shoulder sections using the 3-needle BO. Refer to "Three-Needle Bind Off" on page 13.

Neckband

With RS facing, using the 16" circular needle, K30 (30, 30, 36, 36) sts from the back holder, PU 20 sts along the left front, K20 (20, 20, 26, 26) sts from the front holder, and PU 20 sts along the right front. PM to mark the beg of the rnd—90 (90, 90, 102, 102) sts.

Rnd 1: Purl.

Rnd 2: Knit.

BO pw.

Sleeves

Beg at cuff, CO 43 (43, 47, 47, 51) sts. Work even in patt until sleeve measures 2½ (2½, 3, 3, 3)" from the beg, ending with a WS row. Inc 1 st at each end of the next row and every 4 rows to 95 (95, 101, 101, 109) sts, bringing the new sts into the est patt.

■ **Recommended inc:** *Inc by using the M1 technique **after** the first st of the rnd and another M1 **before** the last st of the rnd. Refer to "Increasing" on page 13.*

Work even in patt until sleeve measures 17 (17, 18, 18, 19)" or the desired length, ending with a WS row. BO.

Finishing

Sew in the sleeves. Sew the underarm and side seams. Weave in all the loose ends.

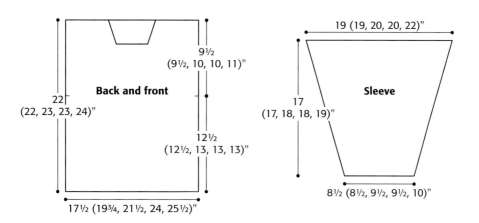

Back and front

22 (22, 23, 23, 24)"

9½ (9½, 10, 10, 11)"

12½ (12½, 13, 13, 13)"

17½ (19¾, 21½, 24, 25½)"

19 (19, 20, 20, 22)"

Sleeve

17 (17, 18, 18, 19)"

8½ (8½, 9½, 9½, 10)"

Inside/Outside Sweater

As I was knitting this sweater, I began to like the wrong side more and more. Consequently, what originally was to be the inside ended up being the outside. You decide which side you prefer and assemble it accordingly. Or, simply make two sweaters for totally different looks inside and outside.

Finished chest measurement: 36 (40, 44, 48, 52)"
Finished length: 22 (22, 23, 24, 24)"
Sleeve drop: 9 (9, 10, 11, 11)"

Materials

Yarn: 5 (6, 7, 8, 9) skeins of 220 from Cascade (3½ oz/220 yds; 100% wool; color 2413) or approx 1100 (1300, 1500, 1700, 2000) yds of worsted-weight yarn ❹

Needles: Straight or 24" circular needles in size 7, or the size required to obtain gauge; 16" circular needle in size 7

Notions: St holders, st markers, row markers

Gauge

5 sts and 7 rows = 1" in patt st on size 7 needles

Back

Using the straight or 24" circular needles, CO 90 (100, 110, 120, 130) sts.

Row 1: P1, K3, *P2, K3, rep from * to last st, P1.

Row 2: Purl.

These 2 rows form the patt. Rep patt until the back measures 22 (22, 23, 24, 24)" from beg or the desired length, ending by working row 2. Divide sts onto 3 st holders as follows:

First and third holders: 30 (35, 38, 43, 46) sts each for shoulders
Second holder: 30 (30, 34, 34, 38) sts for back neck

Front

Work same as the back until the front measures 3" *shorter* than total length of the back, ending with row 2.

Neck Shaping

Work in patt across 35 (40, 45, 50, 55) sts. Place next 20 sts onto a st holder. Attach a 2nd skein of yarn and cont in patt across the rem 35 (40, 45, 50, 55) sts. Working both sides at the same time and keeping in patt, dec 1 st on each side of the neck on the next row and every 2 rows for a total of 5 (5, 7, 7, 9) times—30 (35, 38, 43, 46) sts rem. Work even until the front measures the same as the back, ending by working row 2. Join front and back shoulders tog using the 3-needle BO. Refer to "Three-Needle Bind Off" on page 13.

▊ *At this point you'll have to decide which side you prefer to use as the **right** side of your sweater.*

Neckband

With RS facing, using the 16" circular needle, PU 20 sts along the right front, K20 sts from the front holder, PU 20 sts along the left front, and K30 (30, 34, 34, 38) sts from the back holder. PM to mark the beg of the rnd—90 (90, 94, 94, 98) sts.

Rnd 1: Purl.

Rnd 2: Knit.

Rnd 3: Purl.

Rnd 4: Knit, dec 4 (4, 4, 4, 8) sts evenly across the rnd.

Rnd 5: BO pw.

Sleeves

CO 40 (40, 50, 50, 50) sts. Work in patt as for the back until sleeve measures 3", ending with row 2. Inc at the beg and end of the next row and *every* 4 rows to 90 (90, 100, 110, 110) sts, bringing the new sts into the est patt.

▉ *Recommended inc: Inc by using the M1 technique* **after** *the first st of the rnd and another M1* **before** *the last st of the rnd. Refer to "Increasing" on page 13.*

Cont working even in patt until sleeve measures 17 (17, 18, 18, 18)" from the beg or the desired sleeve length, ending with row 2. BO loosely.

Finishing

Sew in the sleeves. Weave in all the loose ends.

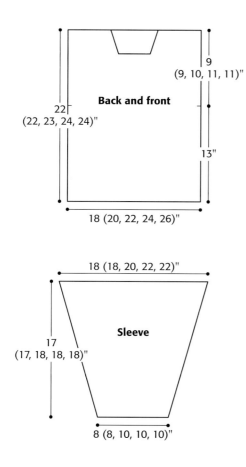

Back and front

9
(9, 10, 11, 11)"

22
(22, 23, 24, 24)"

13"

18 (20, 22, 24, 26)"

18 (18, 20, 22, 22)"

Sleeve

17
(17, 18, 18, 18)"

8 (8, 10, 10, 10)"

Garter Side-to-Side Striped Jacket

Either follow the striping sequence provided or let your creativity go and use your own color choices. This jacket is equally lovely done with leftover yarns from other projects. It is knit starting at the left sleeve cuff. The front and back sections are added onto the completed sleeve sections using a provisional cast on. After dividing for the neck opening, the left front is completed and the left back is worked up to the center. This process is then repeated for the right side. The sweater is finished using the kitchener stitch for the center back seam as well as the side seams. The underarm seams are woven together.

Finished chest measurement: 36 (42, 48, 54, 60)"
Finished length: 24 (24, 24, 24, 24)"
Sleeve drop: 11½ (11½, 12, 12, 12½)"

Materials

Yarn: Pastaza from Cascade (3½ oz/132 yds; 50% llama/50% wool); worsted-weight yarn (4)
   Main color (MC)—530 (650, 790, 960, 1170) yds
   Color A (A)—260 (330, 395, 480, 590) yds
   Color B (B)—260 (330, 395, 480, 590) yds
   Color C (C)—130 (170, 210, 260, 310) yds
(The sample sweater was made using the foll Pastaza colors: MC—008, A—006, B—019, C—001) (5)

Needles: 24" and 36" circular needles in size 9, or the size required to obtain gauge

Notions: St holders, spare circular needle, seven ¾" buttons, size H crochet hook, a small amount of scrap bulky yarn

Gauge

3½ sts = 1" in garter st on size 9 needle

Left Side of the Sweater

Starting at the cuff of the sleeve and using the 24" circular needle, CO 34 (36, 36, 40, 40) sts with the MC. Foll the color sequence given below, work sleeve in garter st and note that row 1 is a RS row. When sleeve measures 3", inc 1 st at the beg and the end of the next RS row and every 4 rows to 80 (80, 84, 84, 88) sts. Cont working even until the sleeve measures 18" or the desired length, ending with a WS row. Do not BO. Set aside.

Color Sequence for the Sleeves

Note that you may not complete all the rows that are listed. The number of rows depends on the size of the sweater you're making. Each number and letter indicates the number of rows and the colors used in the sample sweater. Remember, you may use your own color scheme.

10MC—2A—4B—4MC—2A—2MC—2B—4C—4MC—2C—6A—2B—2A—4MC—2A—4MC—2B—6C—2MC—2A—6MC—4B—6A—4MC—2C—2B—4C—6MC—2A—2MC—4B—2C—4MC

Lazy Day Tunic

Done in the round after completion of the bottom flaps, this loose-fitting tunic sweater is just the thing for those cold winter days. Done with a heavier weight yarn, it definitely is a quick-to-knit design.

Finished chest measurement: 34 (40, 46, 52, 58)"
Finished length: 25 (26, 27, 27, 28)"
Sleeve drop: 9 (9½, 10, 10, 11)"

Materials

Yarn: 4 (5, 5, 6, 7) skeins of worsted-weight wool from Marr Haven (4 oz/210 yds; 100% wool in Green Heather) or 840 (950, 1050, 1260, 1470) yds of a heavy worsted-weight yarn 🔵5

Needles: 29" circular needle in size 9, or the size required to obtain gauge; two 16" circular needles in size 9; dpns in size 9

Notions: St holders, st markers

Gauge

3½ sts and 5 rows = 1" in St st on size 9 needle

Bottom Flaps (make 2)

Using one of the 16" circular needles, CO 60 (70, 80, 90, 100) sts.

Row 1 (RS): Knit.

Row 2: K3, P4, *K1, P4, rep from * across to last 3 sts, K3.

Rep these 2 rows until the bottom flap measures 3 (3, 4, 4, 4)" from beg, ending with a WS row.

On the first flap, cut yarn, leaving a 5" tail, and set the flap aside. Using the second 16" circular needle, make the second flap. *Do not cut the yarn on the second flap.*

Joining Flaps

With the 29" circular needle, knit across the sts on needle from the second flap. PM. Knit the first flap sts onto the same needle as the second flap. PM and join, making sure that you are not twisting the sts. You will now be working in the rnd—120 (140, 160, 180, 200) sts.

Body

Rnd 1: K2, P1, *K4, P1, rep from * to last 2 sts, K2.

Rnd 2: Knit.

Rep these 2 rnds until body measures 16 (16½, 17½, 17, 17)" from the beg, ending by working rnd 2.

Dividing for the Front and the Back

Work in the est patt across 60 (70, 80, 90, 100) sts. Place these sts on a st holder or a spare needle to use later for the sweater front. Work in patt across the rem 60 (70, 80, 90, 100) sts. Turn your work and purl back across these sts. You will now be working back and forth.

Back

Row 1 (RS): K2, P1, *K4, P1. Rep from * across row to last 2 sts, K2.

Row 2: Purl.

Cont working in patt until piece measures 9 (9½, 9½, 10, 11)" from dividing row.

Divide sts onto 3 holders, as follows:
First and third holders: 20 (24, 28, 32, 36) sts each for shoulders
Second holder: 20 (22, 24, 26, 28) sts for back neck

Front

Return the front sts to the needle so that the WS is facing for the first row. Attach the yarn and purl across these sts. Begin working in patt as for back until the front measures 3" *shorter* than total back length. End by working a WS row.

Neck Shaping

Work in patt across 25 (29, 33, 37, 41) sts. Place next 10 (12, 14, 16, 18) sts on a st holder. Attach a 2nd skein of yarn and work in est patt across the rem 25 (29, 33, 37, 41) sts. Work both sides at the same time and cont in patt, dec 1 st at each side of neck edge on *every* RS row for a total of 5 times.

▮ *To make the neckline lie more smoothly and look more uniform, K2tog for the dec at the left neck edge and SSK for the dec at the right neck edge. Refer to "K2tog" and "SSK" on page 13.*

Cont in the est patt for the rem 20 (24, 28, 32, 36) sts until front measures the same as back to the shoulders.

Join the front to the back using the 3-needle BO. Refer to "Three-Needle Bind Off" on page 13.

Neckband

With the RS facing you and starting at the back of the sweater, use a 16" circular needle and K20 (22, 24, 26, 28) sts from the back holder. PU 15 sts down the left front, K10 (12, 14, 16, 18) sts from front holder, and PU 15 sts from the right neck front. PM—60 (64, 68, 72, 76) sts.

Rnds 1 and 3: Purl.

Rnd 2: Knit.

Rnd 4: Knit, dec 4 sts evenly around. BO pw.

Sleeves

Using dpns, CO 30 (30, 35, 35, 40) sts. PM and join, being careful not to twist the sts.

Rnd 1: Knit.

Rnd 2: K2, P1, *K4, P1, rep from * to last 2 sts, K2.

Work even in patt for 3". Cont in patt, inc 1 st at the beg and the end of the next rnd and then every 4 rnds to 64 (66, 71, 71, 78) sts, bringing the new sts into the patt. Switch to a circular needle when there are enough sts to do so.

■ *Recommended inc: Inc by using the M1 technique **after** the first st of the rnd and another M1 **before** the last st of the rnd. Refer to "Increasing" on page 13.*

Work even in patt to 18 (18, 18, 19, 19)" or the desired sleeve length. BO loosely.

Finishing

Sew in the sleeves. Weave in all the loose ends.

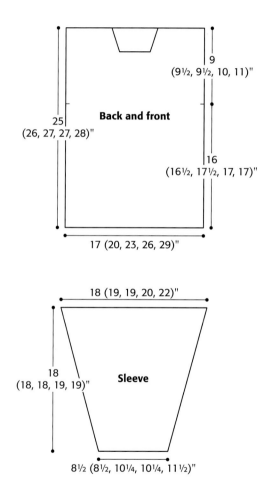

Back and front

9 (9½, 9½, 10, 11)"

25 (26, 27, 27, 28)"

16 (16½, 17½, 17, 17)"

17 (20, 23, 26, 29)"

Sleeve

18 (19, 19, 20, 22)"

18 (18, 18, 19, 19)"

8½ (8½, 10¼, 10¼, 11½)"

Carolina Comfort

The addition of a simple slipped stitch adds extra interest to this basic garter stitch design.

Finished chest measurement: 36 (42, 48, 54, 60)"
Finished length: 23½ (23½, 24, 24½, 24½)"
Sleeve drop: 9½ (9½, 10, 10½, 10½)"

Materials

Yarn: 3 (4, 4, 5, 5) hanks of Carolina from Interlacements (8 oz/310 yds; rayon/cotton/flax; color 106), or approx 1000 (1070, 1140, 1210, 1280) yds of worsted-weight yarn ⑤

Needles: Straight or 24" circular needles in size 7, or the size required to obtain gauge; 16" circular needle in size 7

Notions: St holders, st markers, row markers

Gauge

4 sts and 14 rows = 1" in garter st on size 7 needles

Back

Using the straight or 24" circular needles, CO 71 (83, 95, 107, 119) sts.

Row 1 (RS): Knit.

Row 2: K5, sl 1 wyif, *K11, sl 1 wyif, rep from * across row to last 5 sts, K5.

Rep these 2 rows until back measures 23½ (23½, 24, 24½, 24½)" from beginning or desired length, ending with a WS row. Divide sts onto 3 st holders as follows:

First and third holders: 22 (26, 31, 37, 41) sts each for shoulders

Second holder: 27 (31, 33, 33, 37) sts for back

Front

Work same as the back until the front measures 3" *shorter* than total length of the back, ending with a WS row.

Neck Shaping

Row 1: Work across 31 (36, 41, 47, 52) sts. Place center 9 (11, 13, 13, 15) sts on a st holder, attach a 2nd skein of yarn and work across the rem 31 (36, 41, 47, 52) sts. Working each side simultaneously with separate yarns, cont as foll:

Row 2: Work even in patt across each side.

Keeping in est patt, dec 1 st on each side of neck on next row and *every* RS row 9 (10, 10, 10, 11) times—22 (26, 31, 37, 41) sts rem.

■ *To make the neckline lie more smoothly and look more uniform, K2tog for the dec at the left neck edge and SSK for the dec at the right neck edge. Refer to "K2tog" and "SSK" on page 13.*

Work even until the front measures the same length as the back. Join the front and the back shoulders using the 3-needle BO. Refer to "Three-Needle Bind Off" on page 13.

Neckband

With the RS facing you and using the 16" circular needle, PU 21 (23, 23, 23, 25) sts along the RS of the front neck, K9 (11, 13, 13, 15) from center front holder, PU 21 (23, 23, 23, 25) sts along the left side of front neck, and K27 (31, 33, 33, 37) sts from the back holder. PM—78 (88, 92, 92, 102) sts. You'll now be knitting in the rnd.

Rnd 1: Purl.

Rnd 2: Knit.

Rnd 3: Purl.

Rnd 4: Knit, dec 4 (4, 4, 4, 8) sts evenly across rnd.

Rnd 5: BO pw.

Sleeves

Beg at the cuff, CO 43 (43, 45, 47, 47) sts.

Row 1: Knit.

Row 2: K3 (3, 4, 5, 5), sl 1 wyif, *K11, sl 1 wyif, rep from * across row to last 3 (3, 4, 5, 5) sts, K3 (3, 4, 5, 5).

Work even in patt until sleeve measures 3" from the beg, ending with a WS row. Inc at beg and end of the next row and then every 6 rows to 77 (77, 81, 85, 85) sts. Bring the new sts into the est patt. Cont working in patt until the sleeve measures 18 (18, 18, 19, 19)" or the desired length from the beg, ending with a WS row. BO loosely.

Finishing

Sew in the sleeves. Sew the underarm and side seams. Weave in all the loose ends.

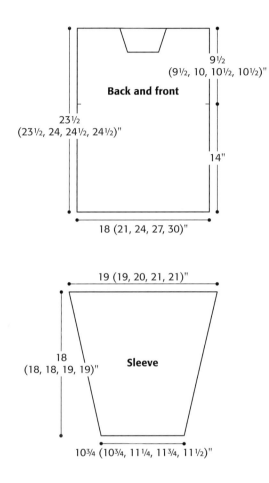

Back and front

9½
(9½, 10, 10½, 10½)"

23½
(23½, 24, 24½, 24½)"

14"

18 (21, 24, 27, 30)"

19 (19, 20, 21, 21)"

Sleeve

18
(18, 18, 19, 19)"

10¾ (10¾, 11¼, 11¾, 11½)"

Basic Pullover

Truly a design to live in, this pullover is sure to be a favorite. Its basic design makes it perfect for casual dressing.

Finished chest measurement: 36 (40, 44, 47, 51, 55)"
Finished length: 26 (27, 27, 28, 29, 30)"
Sleeve drop: 9½ (10, 10, 10½, 11, 11½)"

Materials

Yarn: 13 (15, 16, 17, 19, 20) skeins of Irland from Skacel (1¾ oz/77 yds; 80% wool, 7% rayon, 13% acrylic; color 658) or approx 1000 (1100, 1200, 1300, 1400, 1500) yds of worsted-weight yarn ⟨4⟩

Needles: 29" circular needle in size 7, or the size required to obtain gauge; 16" circular needle in size 7; 29" circular needle in size 5; dpns in size 5; dpns in size 7

Notions: St markers, st holders

Gauge

4½ sts and 6½ rows = 1" in St st on size 7 needle

Body

Using the size 5 circular needle, CO 164 (180, 196, 212, 228, 248) sts. PM and join. Be careful not to twist the sts. Work in K2, P2, ribbing for 1½". Change to the 29" circular needle in size 7 and cont in St st (knit every rnd) until the body measures 16½ (17, 17, 17½, 18, 18½)" from the beg or the desired length to underarm.

Dividing for the Front and the Back

K82 (90, 98, 106, 114, 124) sts. Place the rem sts on a st holder or a spare circular needle to be used later for the front.

Back

Working back and forth, cont in St st (knit on RS, purl on WS) until the back measures 9½ (10, 10, 10½, 11, 11½)" from the dividing row, ending with a WS row. Do not BO. Place sts onto 3 st holders, divided as follows:

First and third holders: 29 (32, 36, 38, 42, 45) sts each for shoulders

Second holder: 24 (26, 26, 30, 30, 34) sts for back neck

Front

With the RS facing you, join the yarn. Work back and forth in St st until the front is 20 (20, 20, 22, 22, 26) rows *shorter* than back, ending with a WS row.

Neck Shaping

K36 (40, 44, 47, 51, 55) sts. Place next 10 (10, 10, 12, 12, 14) sts on a st holder. Attach a 2nd skein of yarn and K36 (40, 44, 47, 51, 55) sts. Working both sides at the same time, cont in St st, dec 1 st at both sides of neck edge on next 10 rows— 26 (30, 34, 37, 41, 45) sts on each side.

■ *To make the neckline lie more smoothly and look more uniform, K2tog for the dec at the left neck edge and P2tog for the dec at the right neck edge. Refer to "K2tog" and "P2tog" on page 13.*

Work 9 (9, 9, 11, 11, 15) rows even, ending with a WS row. Join the front and the back shoulders using the 3-needle BO. Refer to "Three-Needle Bind Off" on page 13.

Neckband

With the RS facing you and using the 16" circular needle, K30 (30, 30, 32, 32, 34) sts from the back st holder onto the needle, PU 20 (20, 20, 22, 22, 22) sts along the left front, K10 (10, 10, 12, 12, 14) sts from the front holder, and PU 20 (20, 20, 22, 22, 22) sts along the right front. PM to mark the beg of the rnd—80 (80, 80, 88, 88, 92) sts. Work in K2, P2 ribbing for 2½". BO loosely in rib.

Sleeves

Using the size 5 dpns, CO 44 (44, 48, 48, 52, 52) sts. PM and join. Be careful not to twist the sts. Work in K2, P2 ribbing for 1½". Change to the size 7 dpns and work in St st while *at the same time* inc 1 st at the beg *and* the end of every 4 rnds to 86 (90, 90, 96, 100, 102) sts.

■ *Switching needles: You can switch to the 16" circular needle when you have enough sts to do so.*

Recommended inc: *Inc by using the M1 technique* **after** *the first st of the rnd and another M1* **before** *the last st of the rnd. Refer to "Increasing" on page 13.*

Work even until the sleeve measures 17 (17, 17, 18, 18, 18)" or the desired length. BO loosely.

Finishing

Sew in the sleeves. Turn neckband ribbing in half to WS and whipstitch the neckband in place. Weave in all the loose ends.

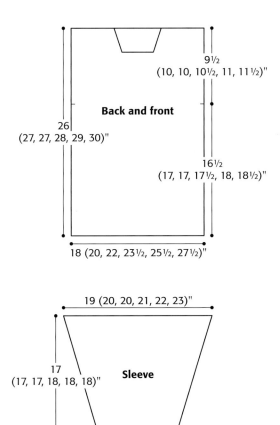

Garter Side-to-Side Solid Jacket

This jacket is a great and simple pattern to use as an introduction to side-to-side knitting.

Finished chest measurement: 36 (42, 48, 54, 60)"
Finished length: 24 (24, 24, 24, 24)"
Sleeve drop: 11½ (11½, 12, 12, 12½)"

Materials

Yarn: 4 (5, 5, 6, 7) skeins of worsted-weight wool from Marr Haven (4 oz/210 yds; 100% wool; Blue Heather) or approx 840 (945, 1050, 1250, 1470) yds of a heavy worsted-weight yarn 🅢

Needles: 24" and 36" circular needles in size 9, or the size required to obtain gauge

Notions: St holders, spare circular needle, seven ¾" buttons, size H crochet hook, a small amount of scrap heavy worsted yarn

Gauge

3½ sts = 1" in garter st on size 9 needle

Left Side of Sweater

Beg at cuff of sleeve and using the 24" circular needle, CO 34 (36, 36, 40, 40) sts. Work 6 rows in garter st, ending with a WS row. Switch to St st. When sleeve measures 3" from beg, inc 1 st at the beg and the end of the next RS row and every 4 rows to 80 (80, 84, 84, 88) sts.

■ *Recommended inc: Inc by using the M1 technique after the first st of the rnd and another M1 before the last st of the rnd. Refer to "Increasing" on page 13.*

Cont working even until sleeve measures 18" or the desired length, ending with a WS row. Do not BO. Set aside.

Left Body

Row 1: Using the provisional CO and scrap yarn, CO 44 sts on the 36" circular needle. With the RS facing you, knit the sleeve sts onto the needle. Using the provisional CO and more scrap yarn, CO an additional 44 sts—168 (168, 172, 172, 176) sts. Refer to "Provisional Cast On" on page 12.

Work even in garter st (knit every row) until the left body measures 6 (7, 8, 9, 10)" from the start of body, ending with a WS row.

Divide for front and back as follows: K82 (82, 84, 84, 86) sts. Place the next 4 sts onto a st holder. Place the rem 82 (82, 84, 84, 86) sts on a large st holder or a spare circular needle to use later for the front.

Back

Work even in est patt until the back measures 9 (10½, 12, 13½, 15)" from the back CO edge, ending with a WS row. Put these sts on a st holder or a spare circular needle.

Left Front

Sl the 82 (82, 84, 84, 86) front sts on a circular needle with the RS facing you for first row.

Rows 1, 3, 5, 7, and 9 (RS): K1, K2tog, knit to the end of row.

Rows 2, 4, 6, 8, and 10: K77 (77, 79, 79, 81) sts. Work even until the left front measures 9 (10½, 12, 13½, 15)" from the front CO edge. Knit 5 more rows. BO on a WS row.

Right Side of Sweater

Rep as for the left side up to the dividing row for the front and the back.

Cont as follows: Knit across 82 (82, 84, 84, 86) sts for right front. Place the next 4 sts on a st holder. Place the rem 82 (82, 84, 84, 86) sts on another st holder or a spare circular needle for the right back.

Right Front

Rows 1, 3, 5, 7, and 9: Knit.

Rows 2, 4, 6, 8, and 10: Knit to last 3 sts, K2tog, K1—77 (77, 79, 79, 81) sts. Work even until the right front measures 9 (10½, 12, 13½, 15)" from the front CO edge, ending with a WS row.

Buttonholes

Row 1: K1 (1, 1, 1, 2), BO next 2 sts, K9 (9, 9, 9, 9), BO next 2 sts, rep from * across to 1 (2, 2, 2, 2) st, K1 (2, 2, 2, 2).

Row 2: K2 (3, 3, 3, 3), CO 2 sts, *K10 (10, 10, 10, 10), CO 2 sts, rep from * across to last 1 (1, 1, 1, 2) st, K1 (1, 1, 1, 2).

Knit 3 more rows. BO kw on the WS.

Right Back

With the RS facing you, join the yarn. Work even until the right back measures 9 (10½, 12, 13½, 15)" from the back CO edge, ending with a WS row. Do not BO.

Finishing

Join the center back seam as well as the side seams tog using the kitchener st. Refer to "Kitchener Stitch" on page 16.

Sew the underarm seams. Weave in all the loose ends. Sew the buttons on the left front to correspond with the buttonholes on the right front.

Neckband

Row 1: With the RS facing you, PU 80 (84, 88, 92, 96) sts around.

Rows 2 and 4: Knit.

Rows 3 and 5: Knit, dec 10 sts evenly around.

BO kw on the WS.

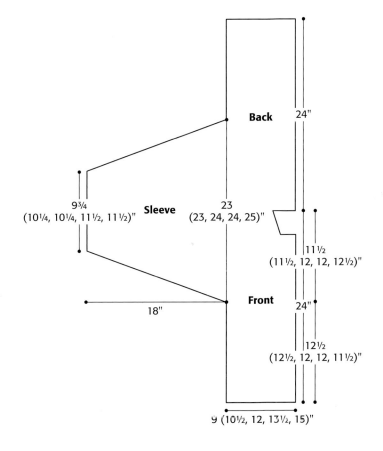

Faux Heart Cardigan

As I was knitting this design using the double moss stitch, a friend kept referring to it as my heart sweater because she thought the design looked like tiny hearts. This has been my faux heart sweater ever since.

Finished chest measurement: 36 (40, 44, 48, 52)"
Sleeve drop: 9½ (9½, 10, 10½, 10½)"
Finished length: 24½ (24½, 25, 25½, 25½)"

Materials

Yarn: 14 (15, 16, 17, 18) skeins of Kathmandu Aran from Queensland Collection (50 g/104 yds; 85% merino wool/10% silk/5% cashmere; color 114) or approx 1400 (1500, 1600, 1700, 1800) yds of worsted-weight yarn

Needles: 29" circular needle in size 7, or the size required to obtain gauge; 16" circular needle in size 7; dpns in size 7; any length circular needle in size 6

Notions: Six ¾" buttons, st markers, st holders, a size G crochet hook

Gauge

4½ sts and 6 rows = 1" in patt st on size 7 needle

Pattern Stitch—Double Moss Stitch

Row 1 (RS): *K2, P2, rep from * across row.

Row 2: *K2, P2, rep from * across row.

Row 3: *P2, K2, rep from * across row.

Row 4: *P2, K2, rep from * across row.

Body

Using the 29" size 7 circular needle, CO 164 (180, 200, 216, 236) sts. Work even in the patt st until the body measures 15" from the beg, ending with a WS row.

Dividing for the Front and the Back

Maintaining the est patt, work 41 (45, 50, 54, 59) sts and sl these sts on a st holder to be used later for the front section, K82 (90, 100, 108, 118) sts, and place the rem 41 (45, 50, 54, 59) sts onto a st holder to be used later for the other front section.

Back

Cont in est patt, work until the section measures 9½ (9½, 10, 10½, 10½)", ending with a WS row. Divide sts onto 3 holders as follows:

First and third holders: 26 (30, 34, 37, 41) sts each for shoulders

Second holder: 30 (30, 32, 34, 36) sts for back neck

Checkerboard Wave Pullover

The stitch combination used in this pullover pattern gives the illusion of a wave. It would be equally striking in a solid color.

Finished chest measurement: 38 (41, 45, 49, 53)"
Finished length: 23 (23, 24, 24, 25)"
Sleeve drop: 9½ (9½, 10, 10½, 10½)"

Materials

Yarn: 6 (6, 7, 7, 8) skeins of Single Worsted from Sandy's Palette (4 oz/190 yds; 85% mohair/15% wool; color #SW-022) or approx 1050 (1140, 1230, 1330, 1480) yds of a worsted-weight yarn (4)

Needles: Straight or 24" circular needles in size 8, or the size required to obtain gauge; 16" circular needle in size 8

Notions: St holders, st markers, row markers

Gauge

4¼ sts and 8 rows = 1" in patt st on size 8 needles

Back

Using the straight or 24" circular needles, CO 80 (88, 96, 104, 112) sts. Knit 2 rows.

Beg patt as follows:

Rows 1, 3, 5, 7, and 8: Knit.

Rows 2, 4, and 6: K2, P4, *K4, P4, rep from * to last 2 sts, K2.

Rows 9, 11, 13, 15, and 16: Knit.

Rows 10, 12, and 14: P2, K4, *P4, K4, rep from * to last 2 sts, K2.

These 16 rows form the patt. Work in patt until the back measures 23 (23, 24, 24, 25)" from the beg, ending with *either* row 8 or row 16. Divide sts onto 3 holders as follows:

First and third holders: 27 (31, 35, 38, 42) sts each for shoulders

Second holder: 26 (26, 26, 28, 28) sts for back neck

Front

Work the same as the back until the front measures 3" *shorter* than finished back length, ending with a WS row.

Neck Shaping

Work in patt across 35 (39, 43, 46, 50) sts. Place next 10 (10, 10, 12, 12) sts on a st holder. Attach a 2nd skein of yarn and cont in patt across rem 35 (39, 43, 46, 50) sts.

Working each side at the same time in the est patt, dec 1 st on each side of the neck edge on next RS row and *every* RS row 8 times—27 (31, 35, 38, 42) sts.

■ *To make the neckline lie more smoothly and look more uniform, K2tog for the dec at the left neck edge and SSK for the dec at the right neck edge. Refer to "K2tog" and "SSK" on page 13.*

Work even in patt until the front measures the same as the back from the beg. Join the shoulder seams tog using the 3-needle BO. Refer to "Three-Needle Bind Off" on page 13.

Neckband

With the RS facing you and using the 16" circular needle, K26 (26, 26, 28, 28) sts from the back st holder, PU 12 along the left front edge, K10 (10, 10, 10, 12) sts from the front st holder, and PU 12 along the right front edge. PM—60 (60, 60, 64, 64) sts.

Rnd 1: Purl.

Rnd 2: Knit.

Rnd 3: Purl.

Rnd 4: Knit, dec 4 sts evenly around.

BO loosely pw.

Sleeves

CO 32 (32, 40, 40, 40) sts. Knit 2 rows. Begin checkerboard patt as for back. Work until the sleeve measures 2" from the beg, ending with a WS row. Inc 1 st at the *beg* and *end* of the next row and every 4 rows to 84 (84, 88, 92, 92) sts, bringing the new sts into the est patt.

■ ***Recommended inc:*** *Inc by using the M1 technique **after** the first st of the rnd and another M1 **before** the last st of the rnd. Refer to "Increasing" on page 13.*

Cont even in patt to 17 (17, 18, 18, 18)" or the desired length, *ending* with row 8 or 16. BO loosely in patt.

Finishing

Sew in the sleeves. Sew the underarm and side seams. Weave in all the loose ends.

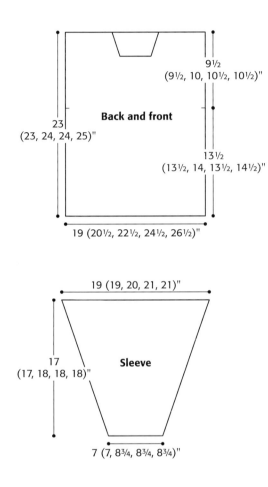

Back and front

9½
(9½, 10, 10½, 10½)"

23
(23, 24, 24, 25)"

13½
(13½, 14, 13½, 14½)"

19 (20½, 22½, 24½, 26½)"

19 (19, 20, 21, 21)"

Sleeve

17
(17, 18, 18, 18)"

7 (7, 8¾, 8¾, 8¾)"

Corded Rib Pullover (DK Version)

This pattern stitch is so easy, yet it looks like it takes lots of concentration to do. I enjoyed the effect so much that I decided to write directions for this sweater in DK-weight as well as worsted-weight yarn.

Finished chest measurement: 34 (36, 38, 41, 45, 48, 50)"
Finished length: 22 (22, 23, 23, 24, 24, 25)"
Sleeve drop: 9½ (9½, 10, 10, 10½, 11, 11)"

Materials

Yarn: 6 (7, 8, 8, 9, 10, 11) skeins of Denim Tweed DK from Sirdar (1¾ oz/186 yds; 60% acrylic/25% cotton/15% wool; color 611) or approx 1100 (1225, 1375, 1525, 1675, 1825, 2000) yds of a DK-weight yarn

Needles: Straight or 24" circular needles in size 5, or the size required to obtain gauge; 16" circular needle in size 5

Notions: St holders, row markers

Gauge

6 sts and 8 rows = 1" in patt st on size 5 needles

Back

Using the straight or 24" circular needles, beg at lower back and CO 101 (108, 115, 122, 136, 143, 150) sts. Work in the double corded rib patt as follows:

Row 1 (RS): *K3, (sl 1 pw, K1, YO, pass slipped st over the K1 and YO) twice, rep from * across row to last 3 sts, K3.

Row 2: K3, *P4, K3, rep from * across row.

These 2 rows form the patt st. Cont working in patt until the back measures 22 (22, 23, 23, 24, 24, 25)" from the beg or the desired length, ending with a WS row. Divide sts onto 3 holders as follows:

First and third holders: 34 (37, 40, 43, 49, 52, 55) sts each for shoulders

Second holder: 33 (34, 35, 36, 38, 39, 40) sts for back neck

Front

Work same as the back until the front measures 3" *shorter* than finished back length, ending with a WS row.

Front Neck Shaping

Work patt across 42 (45, 48, 51, 57, 60, 63) sts. Place the next 17 (18, 19, 20, 22, 23, 24) sts on a st holder. Attach a 2nd skein of yarn and cont in est patt across the rem 42 (45, 48, 51, 57, 60, 63) sts. Working both sides at the same time, begin neck shaping. Dec 1 st at each side of the neck on the next RS row and *every* RS row 8 times—34 (37, 40, 43, 49, 52, 55) sts.

▉ *To make the neckline lie more smoothly and look more uniform, K2tog for the dec at the left neck edge and SSK for the dec at the right neck edge. Refer to "K2tog" and "SSK" on page 13.*

CORDED RIB PULLOVER (DK Version)

Cont to work in patt until the front measures the same as the back, ending with a WS row. Join the front and the back shoulder seams using the 3-needle BO. Refer to "Three-Needle Bind Off" on page 13.

Neckband

Using the 16" circular needle, with the RS of work facing and starting at the left shoulder seam, PU 22 sts along left front, K17 (18, 19, 20, 22, 23, 24) sts from the front holder, PU 22 sts along the right front, and K33 (34, 35, 36, 38, 39, 40) sts from the back holder—94 (96, 98, 100, 104, 106, 108) sts. PM and join.

Rnds 1 and 3: Purl.

Rnds 2 and 4: Knit.

BO pw.

Sleeves

Beg at cuff, CO 52 (52, 59, 59, 59, 66, 66) sts. Work even in double corded rib patt for 2", ending with a WS row. Inc 1 st at the beg and the end of the next rnd and every 4 rnds to 118 (118, 125, 125, 131, 138, 138) sts. You can either bring the inc sts into the est patt or leave them in garter st.

■ **Recommended inc:** *Inc by using the M1 technique* **after** *the first st of the rnd and another M1* **before** *the last st of the rnd. Refer to "Increasing" on page 13.*

Cont to work even until sleeve measures 18 (18, 18, 18½, 18½, 19, 19)" or the desired length, ending with a WS row.

Finishing

Sew in the sleeves. Sew the underarm and side seams. Weave in all the loose ends.

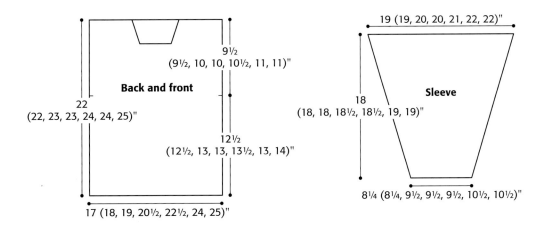

Back and front
9½ (9½, 10, 10, 10½, 11, 11)"
22 (22, 23, 23, 24, 24, 25)"
12½ (12½, 13, 13, 13½, 13, 14)"
17 (18, 19, 20½, 22½, 24, 25)"

Sleeve
19 (19, 20, 20, 21, 22, 22)"
18 (18, 18, 18½, 18½, 19, 19)"
8¼ (8¼, 9½, 9½, 9½, 10½, 10½)"

Corded Rib Pullover (Worsted-Weight Version)

Knit in heavier yarn and on larger needles, this version works up slightly faster than its DK counterpart.

Finished chest measurement: 35 (38, 40, 43, 46, 49, 52)"
Finished length: 22 (22, 23, 23½, 24, 24, 25)"
Sleeve drop: 9½ (9½, 10, 10½, 10½, 11, 11)"

Materials

Yarn: 9 (9, 10, 10, 11, 12, 13) skeins of Kid-N-Ewe from Bryson (3½ oz/120 yds; 50% kid mohair, 50% wool; color 490) or approx 950 (1025, 1100, 1200, 1300, 1400, 1525) yds of a worsted-weight yarn 4

Needles: Straight or 24" circular needles in size 7, or the size required to obtain gauge; 16" circular needle in size 7

Notions: St holders, row markers

Gauge

5 sts and 6 rows = 1" in patt st on size 7 needles

Back

Using the straight or 24" circular needles, beg at lower back and CO 87 (94, 101, 108, 115, 122, 129) sts. Work in the double corded rib patt as follows:

Row 1 (RS): *K3, (sl 1 pw, K1, YO, pass slipped st over the K1 and YO) twice, rep from * across row to last 3 sts, K3.

Row 2: K3, *P4, K3, rep from * across row.

These 2 rows form the patt st. Cont working in est patt until the back measures 22 (22, 23, 23, 24, 24, 25)" from the beg or the desired length, ending with a WS row. Divide sts onto 3 holders as follows:

First and third holders: 29 (32, 35, 38, 41, 44, 47) sts each for shoulders

Second holder: 29 (30, 31, 32, 33, 34, 35) sts for back neck

Front

Work same as the back until the front measures 3" *shorter* than finished back length, ending with a WS row.

Front Neck Shaping

Work in patt across 37 (40, 43, 46, 49, 52, 55) sts. Place next 13 (14, 15, 16, 17, 18, 19) sts on a st holder. Attach a 2nd skein of yarn and work across the rem 37 (40, 43, 46, 49, 52, 55) sts. Working both sides at the same time, begin neck shaping. Dec 1 st at each side of the neck on the next RS row and *every* RS row 8 times—29 (32, 35, 38, 41, 44, 47) sts.

■ *To make the neckline lie more smoothly and look more uniform, K2tog for the dec at the left neck edge and SSK for the dec at the right neck edge. Refer to "K2tog" and "SSK" on page 13.*

Cont to work in patt until the front measures the same as the back. Join front and back shoulder seams using the 3-needle BO. Refer to "Three-Needle Bind Off" on page 13.

Neckband

Using the 16" circular needle, with the RS of work facing you, and starting at the left shoulder seam, PU 18 sts along left front, K13 (14, 15, 16, 17, 18, 19) sts from the front holder, PU 18 sts along the right front, and K29 (30, 31, 32, 33, 34, 35) sts from the back holder—78 (80, 82, 84, 86, 88, 90) sts.

PM and join.

Rnds 1 and 3: Purl.

Rnds 2 and 4: Knit.

BO pw.

Sleeves

Beg at cuff, CO 45 (45, 52, 52, 59, 59, 59) sts. Work even in double corded rib patt for 2", ending with a WS row. Inc 1 st at the beg *and* the end of the next row and every 4 rows to 97 (97, 100, 106, 105, 111, 111) sts. You can either bring the inc sts into the est patt or leave them in garter st.

■ *Recommended inc: Inc by using the M1 technique **after** the first st of the rnd and another M1 **before** the last st of the rnd. Refer to "Increasing" on page 13.*

Cont to work even until the sleeve measures 18 (18, 18, 18½, 18½, 19, 19)" or the desired length, ending with a WS row. BO loosely.

Finishing

Sew in the sleeves. Sew the underarm and side seams. Weave in all the loose ends.

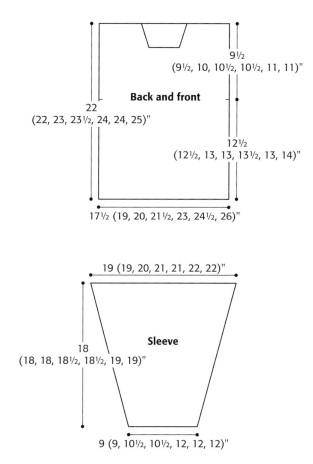

9½
(9½, 10, 10½, 10½, 11, 11)"

Back and front

22
(22, 23, 23½, 24, 24, 25)"

12½
(12½, 13, 13, 13½, 13, 14)"

17½ (19, 20, 21½, 23, 24½, 26)"

19 (19, 20, 21, 21, 22, 22)"

18
(18, 18, 18½, 18½, 19, 19)"

Sleeve

9 (9, 10½, 10½, 12, 12, 12)"

Mock Turtle with a Twist (DK Version)

This basic turtleneck sweater is given an updated look by the simple addition of a decorative ribbing on the bottom of the body and sleeves, as well as on the turtleneck itself. This design has been done in three different weights for you. Pick your favorite yarn weight and make this lovely sweater.

Finished chest measurement: 33 (38, 43, 48, 53)"
Finished length: 24 (25, 26, 27, 28)"
Sleeve drop: 9 (9½, 10, 10½, 11)"

Materials

Yarn: 4 (5, 6, 7, 7) skeins of Soft Touch Wool from Shelridge Farm (3½ oz/275 yards; 100% wool; color—Nutmeg) or approx 1100 (1300, 1500, 1700, 1900) yds of a DK-weight yarn (3)

Needles: 29" circular needle in size 6, or the size required to obtain gauge; 16" circular needle in size 6; dpns in size 6

Notions: St holders, st markers, row markers

Gauge

5½ sts and 7 rows = 1" in patt st on size 6 needle

Body

Using the 29" circular needle, CO 182 (210, 238, 266, 294) sts. PM and join. Be careful not to twist the sts.

Rnd 1: *K3, (sl 1 pw, K1, YO, pass slipped st over the K1 and YO) twice, rep from * around.

Rnd 2: *P3, K4, rep from * around.

These 2 rnds form the corded ribbing patt. Work in est patt for 2½ (2½, 3, 3, 3)".

Change to St st (knit every rnd) and cont until the body measures 15 (15½, 16, 16½, 17)" from the beg, ending with rnd 2.

Dividing for the Front and the Back

Work in the est patt across 91 (105, 119, 133, 147) sts. Place the rem sts onto st holders to be used later for the front section. Turn work; purl back.

Back

You will now be working back and forth. Cont in St st (knit 1 row, purl 1 row) until the back measures 9 (9½, 10, 10½, 11)" from the dividing row. Divide sts onto 3 st holders as follows:

First and third holders: 30 (36, 41, 46, 51) sts each for shoulders

Second holder: 31 (33, 37, 41, 45) sts for back neck

Front

With the RS facing you, return the front sts to the needle. Work in St st until the front measures 3½" *shorter* than the back from the dividing round, ending with a WS row.

Neck Shaping

Work in patt across 40 (46, 51, 56, 61) sts. Place next 11 (13, 17, 21, 25) sts on a st holder. Attach a 2nd skein of yarn and work in est patt across the rem 40 (46, 51, 56, 61) sts.

Working both sides of the neck at the same time, dec 1 st at each neck edge on the next RS row and every RS row 10 times—30 (36, 41, 46, 51) sts.

■ *To make the neckline lie more smoothly and look more uniform, K2tog for the dec at the left neck edge and SSK for the dec at the right neck edge. Refer to "K2tog" and "SSK" on page 13.*

Work even on the rem sts until the front section measures the same as the back from the dividing row.

Join the front shoulders to the back shoulders using the 3-needle BO. Refer to "Three-Needle Bind Off" on page 13.

Neckband

Using the 16" circular needle, with the RS facing you, K31 (33, 37, 41, 45) sts from the back st holder, PU 21 (22, 22, 21, 21) sts along the left neck edge, K11 (13, 17, 21, 25) sts from the front st holder, and PU 21 (22, 22, 21, 21) sts along the right neck edge. PM—84 (90, 98, 104, 112) sts. Knit 1 rnd and inc 0 (1, 0, 1, 0) sts at the center back—84 (91, 98, 105, 112) sts.

Work in the corded rib patt as for sweater bottom for 3", ending with rnd 1. Switch to St st and work an additional 2½". BO loosely kw.

Sleeves

Using dpns, CO 49 (49, 56, 63, 63) sts. PM and join. Be careful not to twist the sts. Work in corded ribbing as for body for 2 (2, 2½, 2½, 2½)", ending with rnd 2.

Switch to St st. Inc 1 st at the beg and the end of the next rnd and every 4 rnds to 99 (105, 110, 115, 119) sts.

■ *Recommended inc: Inc by using the M1 technique **after** the first st of the rnd and another M1 **before** the last st of the rnd. Refer to "Increasing" on page 13.*

Work even until the sleeve measures 17 (17, 17½, 18, 18½)" or the desired length.

Finishing

Fold the neckband in half to the inside and loosely st it into place. Sew in the sleeves. Weave in all the loose ends.

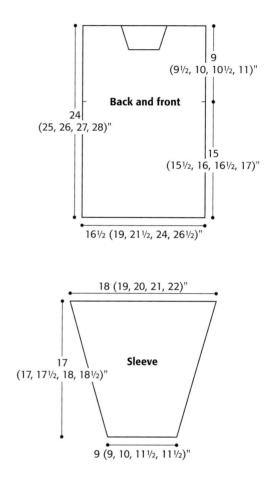

Back and front
24 (25, 26, 27, 28)"
9 (9½, 10, 10½, 11)"
15 (15½, 16, 16½, 17)"
16½ (19, 21½, 24, 26½)"

Sleeve
18 (19, 20, 21, 22)"
17 (17, 17½, 18, 18½)"
9 (9, 10, 11½, 11½)"

Mock Turtle with a Twist (Worsted-Weight Version)

The unique ribbing in this version adds texture to the basic pullover design.

Finished chest measurement: 37 (40½, 43½, 46½, 50)"
Finished length: 24 (25, 26, 27, 28)"
Sleeve drop: 9 (9½, 10, 10½, 11)"

Materials

Yarn: 10 (12, 14, 16, 18) skeins of Alpaca Worsted from Misti (1¾ oz/109 yds; 100% baby alpaca; color #2915) or approx 1000 (1150, 1300, 1500, 1700) yds of a worsted-weight yarn (4)

Needles: 29" circular needle in size 8, or the size required to obtain gauge; 16" circular needle in size 8; dpns in size 8

Notions: St holders, st markers, row markers

Gauge

4½ sts and 6 rows = 1" in patt st on size 8 needle

Body

Using the 29" circular needle, CO 168 (182, 196, 210, 224) sts. PM and join. Be careful not to twist the sts.

Rnd 1: *K3, (sl 1 pw, K1, YO, pass slipped st over the K1 and YO) twice, rep from * around.

Rnd 2: *P3, K4, rep from * around.

These 2 rnds form the corded ribbing patt. Work in est patt for 2½ (2½, 3, 3, 3)".

Change to St st (knit every rnd) and cont until the body measures 15 (15½, 16, 16½, 17)" from the beg, ending with row 2.

Dividing for the Front and the Back

Work in patt across 84 (91, 98, 105, 112) sts. Place rem sts on a st holder to be used later for the front section. Turn work; purl back.

Back

You will now be working back and forth. Cont in St st (knit 1 row, purl 1 row) until the back measures 9 (9½, 10, 10½, 11)" from the dividing round. Divide sts onto 3 st holders as follows:

First and third holders: 28 (31, 34, 37, 40) sts each for shoulders

Second holder: 28 (29, 30, 31, 32) sts for back neck

Front

With the RS facing you, return the front sts to the needle. Work in St st until the front measures 3½" *shorter* than back from the dividing row, ending with a WS row.

70

Neck Shaping

Work in patt across 36 (39, 42, 45, 48) sts. Place next 12 (13, 14, 15, 16) sts onto a st holder. Attach a 2nd skein of yarn and work in est patt across the rem 36 (39, 42, 45, 48) sts.

Working both sides of the neck at the same time, dec 1 st at each neck edge on the next RS row and every RS row 8 times—28 (31, 34, 37, 40) sts.

■ *To make the neckline lie more smoothly and look more uniform, K2tog for the dec at the left neck edge and SSK for the dec at the right neck edge. Refer to "K2tog" and "SSK" on page 13.*

Work even on the rem sts until the front section measures the same as the back from the dividing row.

Join the front and back shoulders using the 3-needle BO. Refer to "Three-Needle Bind Off" on page 13.

Neckband

Using the 16" circular needle, with the RS facing you, K28 (31, 34, 37, 40) sts from the back st holder, PU 22 (21, 22, 23, 22) sts along the left neck edge, K12 (13, 14, 15, 16) sts from the front st holder, and PU 22 (21, 22, 23, 22) sts along the right neck edge. PM—84 (86, 92, 98, 100) sts. Knit 1 rnd, dec 0 (2, 1, 0, 2) sts at center back—84 (84, 91, 98, 98) sts.

Work in the corded ribbing patt as for the sweater bottom for 3", ending with rnd 1. Switch to St st and work an additional 2½". BO loosely kw.

Sleeves

Using dpns, CO 42 (42, 49, 56, 56) sts. PM and join. Be careful not to twist the sts. Work in the corded ribbing patt as for the body for 2½ (2½, 3, 3, 3)", ending with rnd 2.

Change to St st. Knit 2 rnds. Inc 1 st at the beg and the end of the next rnd and every 4 rnds to 82 (86, 91, 96, 100) sts.

■ **Recommended inc:** *Inc by using the M1 technique **after** the first st of the rnd and another M1 **before** the last st of the rnd. Refer to "Increasing" on page 13.*

Work even until the sleeve measures 17 (17, 17½, 18, 18½)" or the desired length.

Finishing

Fold neckband in half to the inside and loosely st into place. Sew in the sleeves. Weave in all the loose ends.

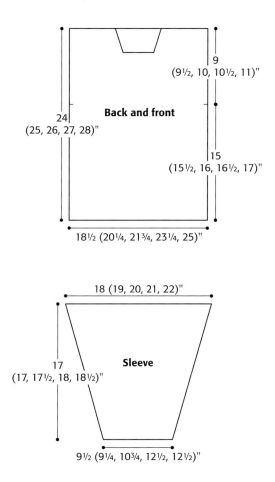

Back and front

9 (9½, 10, 10½, 11)"

24 (25, 26, 27, 28)"

15 (15½, 16, 16½, 17)"

18½ (20¼, 21¾, 23¼, 25)"

Sleeve

18 (19, 20, 21, 22)"

17 (17, 17½, 18, 18½)"

9½ (9¼, 10¾, 12½, 12½)"

Mock Turtle with a Twist (Bulky Version)

Bulky-weight yarn and a large needle give this sweater a casual look. This sweater is perfect for cold days.

Finished chest measurement: 36 (40, 44, 48, 52)"
Finished length: 24 (25, 26, 27, 28)"
Sleeve drop: 9 (9½, 10, 10½, 11)"

Materials

Yarn: 7 (7, 8, 8, 9) skeins of 128 Tweed from Cascade (3½ oz/128 yds; 100% wool; color 7610) or approx 800 (825, 875, 1000, 1200) yds of bulky-weight yarn [5]

Needles: 29" circular needle in size 9, or the size required to obtain gauge; 16" circular needle in size 9; dpns in size 9

Notions: St holders, st markers, row markers

Gauge

3½ sts and 5 rows = 1" in St st on size 9 needle

Body

Using the 29" circular needle, CO 126 (140, 154, 168, 182) sts. PM and join. Be careful not to twist the sts.

Rnd 1: *K3, (sl 1 pw, K1, YO, pass slipped st over the K1 and YO) twice, rep from * around.

Rnd 2: *P3, K4, rep from * around.

These 2 rnds form the corded ribbing patt. Work in the corded ribbing patt for 2½ (2½, 3, 3, 3)", ending with rnd 2. Change to St st (knit every rnd) and cont until the body measures 15 (15½, 16, 16½, 17)" from the beg.

Dividing for the Front and the Back

Work in est patt across 63 (70, 77, 84, 91) sts. Place rem sts on a st holder to be used later for the front section. Turn work; purl back.

Back

You will now be working back and forth.

Cont in St st (knit 1 row, purl 1 row) until the back measures 9 (9½, 10, 10½, 11)" from the dividing row. Divide the sts onto 3 st holders as follows:

First and third holders: 21 (24, 27, 31, 34) sts each for shoulders

Second holder: 21 (22, 23, 22, 23) sts for back neck

Front

With the RS facing you, return the front sts to the needle. Work in St st until front measures 3½ (4, 4, 4½, 4½)" *shorter* than the back from the dividing row, ending with a WS row.

Neck Shaping

Work in est patt across 26 (29, 32, 36, 39) sts. Place next 11 (12, 13, 12, 13) sts on a st holder. Attach a 2nd skein of yarn and cont in est patt across the rem 26 (29, 32, 36, 39) sts.

Working both sides of the neck at the same time, dec 1 st at each neck edge on the next RS row and *every* RS row 5 times—21 (24, 27, 31, 34) sts.

■ *To make the neckline lie more smoothly and look more uniform, K2tog for the dec at the left neck edge and SSK for the dec at the right neck edge. Refer to "K2tog" and "SSK" on page 13.*

Work even on the rem sts until the front section measures the same as the back from the dividing row.

Join the front and back shoulders using the 3-needle BO. Refer to "Three-Needle Bind Off" on page 13.

Neckband

Using the 16" circular needle, with the RS facing you, K21 (22, 23, 22, 23) sts from the back st holder, PU 15 (18, 17, 21, 20) sts along the left neck edge, K11 (12, 13, 12, 13) sts from the front st holder, and PU 15 (18, 17, 21, 20) sts along the right neck edge. PM—62 (70, 70, 76, 76) sts.

Knit 1 rnd, inc 1 (0, 0, 1, 1) st at the center back. Work in the corded ribbing patt as for the sweater bottom for 3", ending with rnd 1. Switch to St st and work an additional 2½". BO loosely kw.

Sleeves

Using dpns, CO 35 (35, 42, 42, 49) sts. PM and join. Be careful not to twist the sts. Work in corded ribbing patt as for the body for 2½ (2½, 3, 3, 3)", ending with rnd 2.

Switch to St st. Work 2 rnds even. Inc 1 st at the beg *and* the end of the next rnd and every 4 rnds to 63 (67, 70, 74, 77) sts.

◾ ***Recommended inc:*** *Inc by using the M1 technique* ***after*** *the first st of the rnd and another M1* ***before*** *the last st of the rnd. Refer to "Increasing" on page 13.*

Work even until the sleeve measures 17 (17, 17½, 18, 18½)" or the desired length.

Finishing

Fold the neckband in half to the inside and loosely st into place. Sew in the sleeves. Weave in all the loose ends.

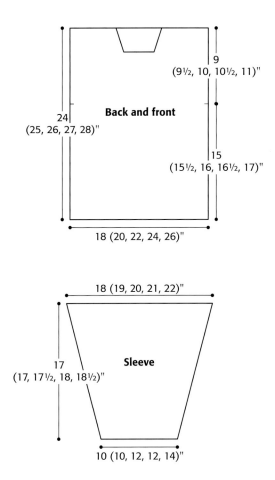

9
(9½, 10, 10½, 11)"

Back and front

24
(25, 26, 27, 28)"

15
(15½, 16, 16½, 17)"

18 (20, 22, 24, 26)"

18 (19, 20, 21, 22)"

17
(17, 17½, 18, 18½)"

Sleeve

10 (10, 12, 12, 14)"

Resources

The following is a list of the companies that supplied yarns and buttons for the projects featured in this book. Their generosity is greatly appreciated. For a list of shops in your area that carry the products mentioned in this book, contact the listed companies.

Bryson Distributing
745 Fillmore
Eugene, OR 97402
www.brysonknits.com

Cascade Yarns
PO Box 58168
Tukwila, WA 98138-1168
www.cascadeyarns.com

Dill Button
50 Choate Circle
Montoursville, PA 17754
www.dill-buttons.com

Interlacements
PO Box 3082
Colorado Springs, CO 80934-3082
www.interlacementsyarns.com

Knitting Fever, Inc.
35 Debevoise Ave.
Roosevelt, NY 11575-0502
www.knittingfever.com
Supplier of Euro Yarns, Noro, and Sirdar

Marr Haven
772 39th St.
Allegan, MI 49010-9353
www.marrhaven.com

Misti International, Inc.
Misti Alpaca Yarns
549 Dorset Ave.
Glen Ellyn, IL 60137
www.mistialpaca.com

Sandy's Palette
1805 Kenneth St.
Madison, WI 53711
www.sandyspalette.com

Shelridge Farm
RR #2 Ariss
Ontario, Canada N0B 1B0
www.shelridge.com

Skacel
PO Box 88110
Seattle, WA 98138
www.skacelknitting.com

About the Author

DOREEN L. MARQUART taught herself to knit at the age of nine after being told she was not teachable because she was left-handed. She distinctly remembers taking yarn, needles, and a knitting how-to book into her parents' bedroom, slamming the door behind her, and claiming she wasn't coming out until she could knit. Three hours later she emerged with knitting hanging from her needles. She's been knitting ever since.

Doreen earned the title of Master Knitter through the Knitting Guild of America in 1998, became a Master Canadian Knitter in 2001, and received the title of Master Canadian Designer in 2002. She has done design work for both Leisure Arts and Cascade Yarns.

Her love of knitting prompted her to open Needles 'n Pins Yarn Shoppe in 1993. From its meager start in a converted one-and-a-half-car garage to its present 1200-square-foot custom-built structure, Needles 'n Pins is now the largest shop in her area devoted exclusively to the needs of knitters and crocheters. Her excitement and enthusiasm for the art of knitting continues to encourage her customers to challenge themselves in their own knitting endeavors.

Doreen lives in the unincorporated southeastern Wisconsin community of Richmond with her husband, Gordon. They have three grown sons—Mike, Phillip, and Cody—and one daughter-in-law, LeAnn. Everyone in Doreen's family has benefited from her passion for knitting and design.

Knitting and Crochet Titles

Martingale® & COMPANY

America's Best-Loved Craft & Hobby Books®
America's Best-Loved Knitting Books®

CROCHET

Classic Crocheted Vests

Crochet from the Heart NEW!

Crochet for Babies and Toddlers

Crochet for Tots

Crocheted Aran Sweaters

Crocheted Lace

Crocheted Socks!

Crocheted Sweaters

First Crochet NEW!

Fun and Funky Crochet NEW!

The Little Box of Crocheted Hats and Scarves

More Crocheted Aran Sweaters NEW!

Today's Crochet

KNITTING

200 Knitted Blocks

365 Knitting Stitches a Year: Perpetual Calendar

Basically Brilliant Knits

Beyond Wool

Big Knitting NEW!

Classic Knitted Vests

Comforts of Home

Dazzling Knits

Fair Isle Sweaters Simplified

First Knits

Garden Stroll, A

Handknit Style

Knit It Now!

Knits for Children and Their Teddies

Knits from the Heart

Knitted Shawls, Stoles, and Scarves

Knitted Throws and More for the Simply Beautiful Home

The Knitter's Book of Finishing Techniques

A Knitter's Template

Knitting with Hand-Dyed Yarns

Knitting with Novelty Yarns

Lavish Lace

The Little Box of Knitted Ponchos and Wraps NEW!

The Little Box of Knitted Throws NEW!

The Little Box of Scarves

The Little Box of Scarves II

The Little Box of Sweaters

More Paintbox Knits

Perfectly Brilliant Knits NEW!

The Pleasures of Knitting

Pursenalities

Rainbow Knits for Kids

Sarah Dallas Knitting

Saturday Sweaters NEW!

Sensational Knitted Socks NEW!

Simply Beautiful Sweaters

Simply Beautiful Sweaters for Men

Style at Large

A Treasury of Rowan Knits

The Ultimate Knitted Tee

The Ultimate Knitter's Guide

Our books are available at bookstores and your favorite craft, fabric, and yarn retailers. If you don't see the title you're looking for, visit us at **www.martingale-pub.com** or contact us at:

1-800-426-3126

International: 1-425-483-3313
Fax: 1-425-486-7596
Email: info@martingale-pub.com

06/05 Knit